I0015202

Manifesting

Sophisticated Methods Of Manifestation For Ceasing
Pursuit, Initiating Attraction, And Cultivating An
Alluring Aura For Your Desired Relationship

*(Acquire The Proficiency In Leveraging The Law Of
Attraction To Embrace Your Aspirations)*

Hartwig Schwaighofer

TABLE OF CONTENT

Introduction

Manifestation involves the process of attracting desired outcomes into one's life through the cultivation of appropriate beliefs. It encapsulates the notion that through unwavering conviction, one has the capacity to manifest a constructive transformation.

Manifestation entails the substantiation of desired outcomes in one's life by means of attraction and a steadfast conviction in their eventual realization. When one materializes the objects of their desires, it serves as a distinct indication that they have deliberately invited them into existence.

The act of materialization can only occur through conviction. One can genuinely bring about every desired aspect of their life, including their ideal professional opportunity, residence, vehicle, and even their perfect life partner.

Prior to acquiring an understanding of the intricacies of manifestation, it is imperative to maintain a receptive mindset, thereby creating ample space for the influx of constructive energies into one's existence.

You harbor remarkable latent abilities that eagerly await activation and unleashing via your cognitive faculties.

There are no bounds to what you can achieve through harnessing the capabilities of your mind. Contemplate the visualized realization of your desired goals, and you shall commence the process of drawing them towards your existence.

One's aspirations determine their identity.

Through the utilization of one's mental capacities, one can attain any desired objective. You can achieve anything you want. When one maintains a positive mindset and emotional disposition towards their aspirations, they will ultimately realize their desired outcome. Through the utilization of mental fortitude, one has the capacity to achieve the desired level of success, aspired for incessantly.

A widespread belief exists among a significant portion of the population that their lives have been predetermined from the moment of their birth. In the event of being born into poverty, they will likely endure a life of impoverished circumstances until their passing. If they were born overweight, they will continue to live in a state of excess weight and ultimately pass away while being overweight. If individuals are born into a state of deep unhappiness, they are likely to persist in that unhappy state throughout their lives, ultimately succumbing to it upon death. We are aware that it is not accurate.

It is my firm conviction that a benevolent deity has orchestrated a promising predetermined fate for every individual. It ultimately pertains to the volition of individuals. One has the potential to become anything one aspires to be. The matter at hand pertains solely to you. You have the capacity to realize your aspirations and attain abundance. Alternatively, you may choose to persist in the belief that success is exclusively attainable by a select few.

Engaging in deliberate contemplation and directing one's attention towards desired objectives. The human intellect is indifferent towards one's desires or aversions. The intellect merely reflects the thoughts and concentration upon which you fixate. The outcome is likely to align with your thoughts and concentration. Thus, deliberating and directing your attention towards your true desires.

Feel good when thinking about your dream. The sentiment you experience dictates whether your aspiration will come to fruition or not. If one experiences positive emotions while contemplating their aspirations, their desires shall materialize. If you are not feeling well, I would recommend engaging in the previously discussed exercise routine.

What is your desired occupation or professional aspiration? An individual who consistently expresses discontent and leads a distressed existence. Alternatively, someone who assumes responsibility for their own life? You have the freedom to determine your chosen path. What is your desired occupation? What is it that you desire to do? What is it that you desire to possess? Do not hesitate to embrace change. The thoughts or opinions of others hold no relevance or significance. It is within your purview to make the determinations regarding the aspirations you have for your own life.

One's thoughts, emotions, and aspirations determine their true identity.

Garbage In Garbage Out

Your thought processes resemble those of a computer. Your subconscious mind manifests the instructions that you imprint upon it. Garbage In Garbage Out. Your conscious thoughts manifest precisely as they are deposited into your subliminal consciousness.

Please take careful note of this information. The thoughts and beliefs that you instill in your subconscious mind have a direct impact on your mental processes and actions. This signifies that regardless of one's wants or desires, the mind carries out precisely what is instilled within the subconscious. Your cognitive faculties have a tendency to draw or materialize the contents of your subconscious mind, irrespective of your conscious wishes. A considerable number of individuals lack comprehension regarding this matter.

The Law of Attraction asserts that similar entities have a tendency to be drawn towards one another. Your thoughts and feelings have the propensity to draw in similar circumstances, ascribed to the workings of your mind. The events that occur in your life are a result of your magnetic influence on them. You bear accountability for the outcomes and events that transpire within the context of your existence.

Upon hearing this, a multitude of individuals converge to voice their disapproval, stating, "Are you insinuating that I am the primary cause of calamity, destitution, affliction, and misfortune befalling me?" Are you implying that I am the one accountable for it?"

Indeed, the reply is affirmative. It is unequivocally you who is responsible for the offense. You are the individual who exemplifies it. You are solely accountable for the outcomes and events that transpire in your life.

They persist in expressing their dissent, asserting, "It is implausible! I refuse to believe that I attract misfortune, wretchedness, illness, and destitution into my existence." I absolutely refuse to allow such an occurrence to transpire in my life! Under no circumstances am I the harbinger of it!"

Indeed, the response is affirmative. It is inconceivable that one would desire to invite calamity, distress, infirmity, and destitution into their life. People harbor an aversion towards the occurrence of calamity, unhappiness, sickness, and destitution in their lives.

However, it is inconsequential what your wants or desires may be, as your subconscious mind solely carries out the programming it has received. The content that is embedded within your subconscious mind will have a profound impact on your cognitive processes, emotional states, and behavioral tendencies. As previously ascertained, one's thoughts and emotions have a direct influence on their state of being. Your cognitive processes give rise to the manifestation of your thoughts and emotions.

A phobia exemplifies an instance wherein an individual's thoughts, emotions, and actions are governed by an underlying subconscious programming. A female individual with a feather phobia acknowledged the occurrence of abandoning her child upon encountering birds or feathers.

If one is afflicted by a phobia, they will invariably abstain from approaching or coming into proximity with the object or situation that triggers their profound anxiety. You shall refrain from approaching it. If you are inherently inclined to experience fear towards something, you will indeed manifest that fear, even if, on a conscious level, you perceive it to be groundless. It is equivalent to both success and failure.

An erroneous programming occurrence that frequently arises pertains to monetary matters. Similar to a phobia, a considerable number of individuals possess an inherent disposition to harbor fear towards monetary matters. I am confident that during your formative years, you may have encountered statements akin to the following: "The love of money is the root of all evil," or "Wealthy individuals possess negative qualities and exploit others," or "The acquisition of wealth distances one from spiritual fulfillment." As a child, you did not undertake an analysis of its veracity. The information that was assimilated by your subconscious mind has been ingrained as a governing mechanism, compelling you to perpetually refrain from pursuing financial gain, unless you make a conscious effort to alter it.

Exploring The Phenomenon Of Manifestation Through The Practice Of Relaxation And Its Associated Advantages

Typically, individuals endeavor to attain their objectives, pursue tangible outcomes, and satisfy their aspirations through diligent and persistent effort. You dedicate ample amounts of time, exertion, vitality, and financial resources towards achieving your goals and enhancing the quality of life for both yourself and your cherished companions. While this method occasionally assists in achieving materialistic aspirations, it is detrimental to one's mental well-being. Your mind and soul perpetually yearn for peace, serenity, and a profound sense of satisfaction, which eludes you due to your unwavering commitment to pursuing greater achievements. The issue at hand pertains to the methodology you employed.

You believe that relentlessly devoting oneself with unwavering effort is the sole means to achieve one's ambitions in life. To your commendation, you are mistaken. By exerting less effort and decreasing your current level of activity, you can accomplish all of your aspirations and yearnings in life. One may achieve their goals through cultivating a state of relaxation, tranquility, serenity, and appreciation. Indeed, your understanding is completely accurate. Please allow us to further explore this concept in order to gain a more comprehensive understanding.

Comprehending the Functioning of Your Cognitive Processes

The realization of a desired outcome does not inherently require extensive labor, the burning of midnight oil, or the depletion of one's physical and mental energy. Once you develop a comprehensive understanding of the processes through which things are brought into existence, as well as the fundamental element that underlies the realization of both material and aspirational objectives, you will inevitably find yourself disinclined to return to your former, frenzied way of living.

The core of all occurrences and internal processes resides within the realm of one's thoughts. Indeed, it is only through one's thoughts and unwavering conviction in them that the unfolding of all matters, whether favorable or unfavorable, comes to fruition. Allow us to provide you with an illustrative example in order to enhance your understanding and facilitate comprehension. Consider the scenario where you find yourself deprived of a significant employment opportunity. In light of encountering this setback, it is probable that you may perceive yourself as a failure or harbor doubts regarding your ability to attain future accomplishments. If you allow this idea to flourish, it gains momentum. In due course, one finds oneself becoming deeply absorbed in this notion and forsaking all other matters. Due to your unwavering conviction in your own culpability for the loss incurred, you fostered the growth of that thought. It is worth noting that thoughts possess the ability to traverse and intermingle with one another. Ideas possess an inclination to draw comparable ideas, prospects, and individuals into one's sphere of influence. Therefore, if one harbors negative thoughts, one inevitably attracts negative outcomes unto oneself. The law of attraction represents a crucial principle that governs the mechanics of the universe. Therefore, if you believe that you exert substantial effort yet struggle to monetize your ideas and attain the long-standing success you aspire to, it is attributable to your detrimental thought patterns.

On the contrary, a constructive mindset facilitates personal growth and advancement without necessitating excessive effort or action. When one adopts a positive mindset, there is a subsequent increase in feelings of personal well-being and self-assurance. This sense of confidence imbues you with the fortitude to advance and make pivotal decisions. Furthermore, the optimistic notion roams the cosmos, diligently searching for favorable and significant opportunities that can effectively contribute to the realization of your objectives. When favorable opportunities present themselves, you have the ability to capitalize on them and bring forth triumph, affluence, prosperity, and joy into your life.

The foundation of bringing about outcomes through relaxation lies in adopting a positive mindset and applying mindful use of one's thoughts.

What is the definition of peaceful manifestation?

It is universally acknowledged that by calming one's mind, there emerges the capacity to discern between detrimental thoughts and beneficial ones. This facilitates the ability to identify pessimistic thoughts and gradually eradicate them from your consciousness. By eliminating the prevalence of unproductive thoughts within your mind, it can subsequently allocate greater capacity for the cultivation of positive thoughts. When one harbors optimistic thoughts within their consciousness, a state of serenity gradually encompasses both their mental faculties and physical being. By achieving a state of mental relaxation and inner peace, one possesses the capability to materialize one's aspirations and attract remarkable opportunities into one's life.

Therefore, by effecting a shift in your mentality and convictions towards the positive, you will be empowered to harness the full potential of your innermost reservoir - your subconscious faculty. The potential of your subconscious mind is truly beyond comprehension. When an action is performed or a memory is formed, that specific piece of information is archived within your subconscious mind. While individuals employ their conscious faculties to perform mundane tasks, it is within their subconscious that resides a repository of knowledge upon which they rely for initiating any course of action. In addition, it is your subconscious mind that possesses the ability to generate and analyze thoughts. Consequently, any thoughts that you perceive originate from your subconscious mind. This implies that by conditioning your subconscious mind to align its thoughts with a positive trajectory, and effectively leveraging pertinent memories and stored knowledge, you can propel yourself towards unparalleled strength, influence, ingenuity, and triumph. One can utilize its potential to conquer fears, enhance strengths, address weaknesses, confront diverse challenges, unleash innate resilience, foster creative capabilities, and strive for personal excellence.

Therefore, the act of materializing one's desires through tranquility and serenity entails accessing one's subconscious gradually in order to harness its potency in facilitating the manifestation of one's desired outcomes. Whether it be an abundance of resources, financial prosperity, optimal well-being, flourishing relationships, the companionship of a significant other, spiritual fulfillment, or any desire that resonates with you, achieving it is within your grasp by simply cultivating a state of relaxation and harnessing the potential of your thoughts and subconscious mind.

Advantages of Manifestation via Relaxation

Now that you have acquired a rudimentary comprehension of the process of manifestation through relaxation, allow us to delve into its significant advantages so as to evoke a true sense of motivation within you to engage in this remarkable method and attain its numerous benefits.

Minimize the Impact of Stress on Your Well-being

Employing the principle of unwavering diligence to attain one's desires yields a significant burden of stress upon an individual. Due to the influence of numerous external factors beyond your control, you experience feelings of stress when you are unable to achieve perfect and desired outcomes. The experience of excessive pressure has the potential to evolve into diverse emotional disorders, such as depression, in a short span of time. Therefore, your demanding and packed itinerary provides little beyond anxiety and strain.

In contrast to this, the act of materializing things through the power of your thoughts is an exceedingly tranquil and serene process. It does not require you to toil diligently or expend extensive time within the confines of the workplace among numerous documents. The only thing that is necessary for you is to attain a state of mental tranquility, thereby enhancing your comprehension of your thoughts and harnessing them for improvement. Therefore, the practice of expressing oneself through relaxation serves as an exemplary means to alleviate the inevitable stressors that permeate one's existence.

Straightforward Process

The process of utilizing peace to achieve your objectives is a remarkably uncomplicated and direct undertaking. It does not entail any complexities or convoluted methodologies. You simply must have faith in yourself, cultivate positive thoughts, and have unwavering belief in their efficacy. That concludes the process! By simply following these steps, you can attract extraordinary opportunities into your life.

Achieve satisfaction with your current possessions

The act of expressing oneself peacefully not only allows for the realization of one's objectives, but also imparts the wisdom of finding contentment and gratitude for the abundant blessings bestowed upon us by the vast universe and the journey of life. As one gains introspection into their thoughts and experiences, they commence recognizing the multitude of aspects that they unwittingly overlook and fail to duly value. This allows you to recognize and appreciate the blessings that you have been given. Through this practice, you begin to cultivate contentment with the blessings you have received and commence earnestly acknowledging and appreciating the benevolence of the universe. When you express gratitude to the universe, it exhibits increased benevolence towards you and reciprocates by manifesting exceedingly positive circumstances in your life.

Attainment of Serenity and Enhanced Standard of Living

By purging your mind of negative thoughts, you can cultivate a favorable mindset that empowers you to discern opportunities amidst almost any circumstances. One begins to discover beams of optimism within even the most despairing circumstances, ultimately finding contentment with one's current circumstances. Additionally, you begin to embrace and accept yourself as you are, while also demonstrating a firm dedication to self-improvement and personal development. As one begins to implement positive changes in their life and resolves any grievances they may have, a gradual attainment of inner peace ensues. When one achieves a state of inner tranquility, there is an observed enhancement in the overall quality of one's existence.

Remarkable indeed! The myriad of significant advantages is truly impressive, wouldn't you agree? To partake in these experiences as well, it is imperative that you proceed to the subsequent chapter in order to embark upon your expedition of manifestation through serenity and tranquility.

Watch your thoughts

Your ideology is the product of your cognitive processes. As previously elucidated, absolute control over one's subconscious mind through meticulous regulation of every individual thought is an unattainable feat. However, what you are able to do is observe and monitor your prevailing thoughts. If you catch yourself thinking of something that is negative, then you have to shift to positive thoughts. Should you find yourself engaging in complaints, indulging in negative thoughts, or fixating on constraints and difficulties, it is imperative for you to redirect your mindset towards a more optimistic perspective. As an illustration, instances arise where you find yourself engrossed in contemplation of issues. The ability to promptly redirect your focus towards your aspirations, desires, and the resolution is conducive in channeling your energy effectively.

Another method for censoring one's thoughts is to be mindful of one's emotions. As we have discussed in the previous chapter, the emotions we experience are the result of the combined effect of our thoughts and beliefs. If you are experiencing sadness or loneliness, it is probable that your current thoughts are focused on negative aspects. Promptly redirect your cognitive focus towards a more optimistic subject. When you direct your attention towards your aspirations, preferences, or genuinely satisfying activities, you will experience an instant enhancement in your well-being. You will feel happier.

The practitioners of Himalayan mysticism and esteemed spiritual guides have attained a profound understanding of mental manipulation through their dedicated daily practice of meditation. They dedicate approximately 30 minutes to one hour solely to introspect and contemplate their thoughts. Certain individuals of a spiritual inclination have attained mastery in the discipline of meditation and manipulation of the mind.

A technique imparted by mystical practitioners to novices involves directing one's attention towards the core of a flower. Every morning, allocate approximately 15 minutes to fix your gaze upon the core of a flower and concentrate your attention on it. When your thoughts become distracted, refocus them onto the core essence of the blossom. This exercise will enhance your ability to exert control over one's thoughts and actions. Furthermore, this activity serves as a means of facilitating mental clarity and inducing a state of tranquility. By engaging in consistent daily practice of this and various other meditation techniques, you will eventually attain full control over your subconscious mind.

Certain practitioners of spiritual mysticism make use of mantra meditation or engage in the cognitive practice of repeatedly reciting affirmations within one's mind. This exercise aims to enhance your belief system and facilitate a transformative shift in your mindset, from a negative perspective to a more positive one.

It is imperative to bear in mind that although your subconscious mind influences the outcome of your life, it is within your capacity to achieve control and expertise over your subconscious faculties. One's mind has the potential to assume control, thereby leading individuals to be ensnared by negative or self-defeating intentions and passively assimilate any incoming information. In the occurrence of this event, you are rendered devoid of any capability or means. Nevertheless, should you attain mastery over your cognitive faculties and possess the ability to exert authority over your mental processes, you would harness its potential to materialize the aspirations that lay deep within your being. Your subconscious mind will engender affirmative resonances that will harmonize with external resonances that align with the corresponding frequency. These vibrational frequencies, energetic manifestations, and universal forces shall collaborate intricately to facilitate the attainment of your desired objectives and wishes.

Empathizing Spiritual Energy Fluctuations

All entities within the sphere of the tangible realm consist of fluctuations in vitality. The fluctuations in vitality can be characterized as oscillating frequencies of information. This revelation is not definitively established in investigative terms; it is primarily pure speculation and conjecture. However, for the purpose of this investigation, let us consider the hypothesis that all entities within your environment, whether perceivable or imperceptible, are comprised of these oscillating frequencies of consciousness. All entities within the cosmos consist solely of oscillating energy forces. This fundamental energy permeates everything within the universe, thereby eradicating any divisions among entities—particularly at the subatomic level. We are interconnected in this manner; we share a common essence wherein we exist as a singular, inseparable entity that is perpetually interwoven.

Scientific evidence has proven that vitality cannot be annihilated; however, it can profoundly alter its composition. This holds utmost importance to acknowledge due to the implication that if everything in our realm consists of energy, then said energy will never merely dissipate, but rather undergo transformation. This consequently gives rise to the conjecture that death does not signify "the end", but rather an "alteration". Nevertheless, it is not solely material objects that possess an energetic imprint. Each element possesses a unique energetic imprint, encompassing not just physical elements, but also intangible entities like thoughts and emotions. The thoughts and emotions that you experience daily emit waves of energy and life throughout the world. This vitality mark can be measured as either being low or high on a vibrational various leveled scale.

The world is founded upon complete opposites. It is admirable and it is appalling; there exists accuracy and there is absence of correctness; there is fondness and there is contempt; there is brightness and there is obscurity; there is illumination and there is dimness. Similarly, the energy within our surroundings can either manifest with heightened intensity or exist at a diminished level. According to popular belief, we attract similar energy or life force into our existence. Therefore, positive thoughts and emotions will attract favorable circumstances, whereas negative thoughts and emotions will attract unfavorable circumstances.

When your energy vibrations are high, it indicates that you are acquiring life-force energy. Additionally, as you cultivate the drive for a fulfilling life, you naturally attract outcomes, situations, individuals, events, and emotions that align with your optimistic aspirations. On the contrary, when your vitality frequencies are diminished, it signifies a depletion of vital energy. Furthermore, in times of being disoriented, one tends to gravitate towards situations, individuals, occurrences, and emotions that align with such diminished energetic frequencies and aspirations. Consequently, this predisposition may potentially lead to illness and adversity.

This vitality is impartial towards goodness or badness, righteousness or wrongdoing, or positivity or negativity.

It is as it is and attracts things that are aligned with those frequencies. These frequencies coincide with the level of affliction and bliss you experience on a daily basis. When you are experiencing distress, you are simultaneously anticipating low-frequency energies. However, when you experience joy, you are immediately anticipating elevated levels of energy. Moreover, within this celestial body, there is a natural tendency for objects to be attracted towards one another. As a result, affliction engenders further suffering, while happiness begets greater bliss. This occurs due to the fundamental cause, as the profound energies surrounding you constantly strive for equilibrium.

When you experience an emotion, you are immediately anticipating a specific energy pattern being projected into the world. The energy and vibrancy ought to be reinstated and permeate the emptiness left behind by its departure. Furthermore, it consistently occupies this vacuum with an equivalent manifestation of energy. In light of this, should you engage in an act fueled by dissatisfaction or fury, it is highly probable that you will encounter situations and events that align with such intensity. Furthermore, consequently, you might find yourself experiencing discomfort or apprehension. You experience these emotions as they share a comparable level of intensity to frustration and anger.

Communication #5 Your Passions Are Sacred – It is Time to Let Go of Anxiety, Regret, and Disgrace!

Many individuals possess a fervent aspiration to materialize their desires, yet they impede their own progress and forego any attempts at actualizing their aspirations. They promptly inhibit themselves once they become aware of or express their inclination.

The reason? Well, they feel guilty. Alternatively, individuals may even experience feelings of embarrassment regarding their aspirations.

It is akin to experiencing a desire while simultaneously harboring negative emotions regarding it. In what way can one cultivate constructive emotions and harmonious behaviors to bring about desired outcomes, while abstaining from engaging in self-deprecating thoughts and behaviors that hinder progress?

In our capacity as your celestial messengers, our purpose is to incite and embolden you. Let go of any sentiments of shame or remorse pertaining to your aspirations. Please acknowledge that the desires that reside within your heart have been bestowed upon you with purpose. They are rightfully meant to be fulfilled by you. They serve as your internal navigational system. Your aspirations are intended to serve as a compass in navigating your path. When employing the term 'journey,' we are not simply alluding to your venture towards manifestation or the instance in which you attain your objectives and fulfill your aspirations.

We are alluding to the voyage of oneself. The process of realizing and actualizing your innate capabilities to attain optimal self-expression and personal growth.

As an illustration, Elena harbored an intense yearning to engage in the pursuit of writing. And we assure you that it proved considerably challenging to establish effective communication with her. On numerous occasions, we attempted to bring to her attention her genuine desires and aspirations, yet she was unresponsive. Instead, she persistently pursued peculiar business opportunities that veered away from her innate calling and true passions.

It required multiple years of diligent effort to help her comprehend and embrace her genuine vocation. We were required to facilitate the development of her self-trust. Since she did not perceive herself as being deserving enough to pursue her aspirations. She harbored a sense of obligation to undertake actions that would render her more deserving of pursuing her passion for writing.

However, upon careful consideration, it becomes evident that the opportune moment to pursue any endeavor is at present, in the current day. Today marks the beginning of your journey.

If you have the desire to impart your expertise or communicate your passion to others, it would be beneficial to cease your concerns and the projection of apprehensions and negative speculation.

Instead, pose the following inquiry unto yourself: If I were to commence my endeavors on this very day, wholeheartedly pursuing my true passion and engaging in that which brings me utmost joy, what transformations shall my life undergo within the span of a year? What is your perspective on the matter in consideration of a timeframe of five years in the future? Alternatively, ten years down the line?

The majority of individuals tend to adhere to an all-or-nothing mindset, whereby they direct their attention towards making excuses rather than centering their efforts on manifesting their desires.

Perhaps this endeavor is not suited to my abilities or interests.

Your rational faculties may attempt to dissuade you from pursuing the aspirations of your heart.

Alternatively, one may become excessively engrossed in ceaseless scholarly inquiry, foregoing the pursuit of personal passions and inclinations, and instead succumbing to the sway of external perspectives.

Might it not be more advantageous to allocate the considerable amount of time expended on worrisome thoughts and negative emotions towards pursuing one's passion and engaging in activities that bring joy and fulfillment?

Indeed, we comprehend your terrestrial responsibilities. We have expressed that it is not necessary for a complete and immediate commitment from the very beginning.

To commence and perpetuate progress, all that is necessary is to grant yourself permission to begin and maintain a steady momentum by consistently advancing in small increments. Keep going.

As an illustration, there exists a profound longing among numerous individuals with imaginative and introspective inclinations to engage in the written word, visual arts, artistic pursuits, or the dissemination of thoughts and feelings through various digital platforms. Numerous individuals achieve remarkable financial success by passionately pursuing their chosen profession. Indeed, it is feasible!

Indeed, we acknowledge that the development of Rome did not occur hastily or overnight. In the current state of existence, phenomena materialize with immediate effect. However, in the context of Earth, there is a delay in the manifestation of things.

But suppose it was consistently effortless for you. What if you had the ability to instantaneously materialize your desires, similar to the manner in which it occurs in our existing realm?

Regrettably, your cognitive faculties would struggle to apprehend it. Moreover, your sense of drive and motivation to pursue fresh objectives and materialize novel endeavors would diminish. Frequently, contentment would not be attained. Therefore, we can only convey to you that circumstances are organized with purpose. It is ultimately for your benefit!

In order to facilitate your empowerment and enable you to confidently embark on motivated endeavors, it is important for you to understand that significant progress can be achieved at a rapid pace when you diligently align your mindset and seamlessly embody your aspirations. Kindly take the time to revisit the section pertaining to the embodiment. Harness your drive and enthusiasm to invigorate the power of purpose by initiating action and pledging to remain authentic to oneself.

Presently, we are able to perceive certain apprehensions that you may hold, particularly in relation to pursuing your passion in a professional capacity.

It is within our comprehension that you may be contemplating:

However, I am concerned about how I will be able to generate an income as I have the responsibility of providing for my family.

- "What if the outcome is unfavorable?"

What if my actions do not receive favor from others and result in a tarnishing of my reputation?

The solution is quite straightforward. It does not pertain to jeopardizing your financial stability or the welfare of your family. The process entails maintaining a steady and cohesive approach towards pursuing one's aspirations, while conceptualizing it as a navigational tool that leads to extraordinary destinations. A location that might bewilder your understanding at present.

As an illustration, in the event that you aspire to articulate your thoughts through the medium of writing, videos, blogs, or social media platforms, or if your aspirations lean towards becoming a mentor or a content creator on YouTube, it is essential to introspect by posing the following inquiry:

May I allocate a minimum of thirty minutes each day?

We have confidence in your ability to do so.

In addition, you have the flexibility to maintain your current employment or fulfill any other commitments you may have.

Don't make any projections. Merely proceed in accordance with your inclination. If it resides within your heart, it was intentionally bestowed upon you. It need not necessarily serve as your ultimate destination. It may serve as the subsequent stage that propels you to a different destination.

Put your trust in the celestial beings and the cosmic forces that govern our existence.

It is conceivable that your newfound aspiration may serve as an indication to initiate concerted efforts to enhance your personal qualities and cultivate discipline. Perhaps it could be interpreted as an indication that may guide you towards acquiring new knowledge?

Always respect and value the insights attained through intuition and the yearnings of your heart.

Rest assured, we possess a high degree of patience and understanding, and thus, we will take the time to explain all of this to you. Elena was difficult. Very stubborn. The sheer magnitude of effort exerted to assimilate her fervor and maintain a harmonized, steadfast course of action is beyond your wildest conception.

In all honesty, it must be acknowledged that we required her presence as a means to disseminate our message and contribute towards elevating the vibrational frequency of our planet. Considering our industry's nature, it became imperative for us to fulfill our responsibilities. Our commitment was driven by our genuine desire and sense of duty, and in the end... we have succeeded in doing so!

It was indeed a formidable task to consistently transmit a multitude of signals and intuitive insights to Elena over the course of numerous years. Despite enduring prolonged periods of neglect, we persevered in our endeavors.

Because we believed. We maintained unwavering confidence in ourselves, our purpose, and our determined young

Elena. Furthermore, we recognized the imperative of persistently demonstrating our commitment by consistently progressing toward our objectives.

Listen attentively to the inner voice of your conscience. It will assist in alleviating the apprehensions residing within your psyche. Please be reminded that you are in a secure environment, surrounded by care and shielded from harm. You have the freedom to retain your identity and carry out your daily routine without any alterations. You are still able to continue your customary professional or daily occupation. And you may continue to progress towards your aspirations.

The Cosmos harbors favor towards expeditiousness, assurance, and unwavering dedication.

Therefore, I implore you to contemplate: "What actions can I undertake today to make progress?"

Now that you have come to perceive your aspiration as a celestial and untainted compass, intended to lead you, do you possess the readiness to proceed accordingly?

Ignite your passion with deliberate intention.

The term "intention" can be understood as incorporating the concept of being "in tension." This notion arises from the initial stages of embarking on an endeavor, wherein one is likely to experience a sense of tension. However, the source of this tension is solely within your thoughts, and you possess the capability to swiftly alleviate it. Maintain your concentration on your internal navigation system and proceed with composure by steadily advancing step by step.

Have faith in yourself and have trust in the cosmic forces of the Universe. Your heart always knows. And we assure you that your celestial beings might experience some fatigue following numerous unsuccessful endeavors to establish communication with you and infuse your inner compass with your authentic aspirations.

The time is now. Let's go!

In the forthcoming chapter, we will impart comprehensive knowledge regarding the process of undertaking necessary actions. We strongly believe that numerous individuals within the manifesting and LOA community would greatly benefit from it, given the prevalent misinterpretations associated with proactive behavior.

How To Utilize The New Age Approach In Crafting Your Law Of Abundance Checks

First: Retrieve a check from your checkbook or generate a new check.

Step Two: In the section titled "Payee," kindly inscribe your complete and official legal name.

Proceed to record the date

Step Four: Consider the specific monetary objective you wish to realize, whether it be the sum required to fulfill a financial commitment or the amount necessary for a pleasurable holiday. Select a sum that exudes a sense of opulence while maintaining feasibility; a sum that can genuinely be envisioned as being acquired within the subsequent 30-day period.

Please transcribe the designated monetary value in the "pay exactly" section.

Procedure Five: Within the designated space for memos, it is permissible to indicate phrases such as 'exceeding anticipated revenue', 'complete payment rendered', or similar content.

Proceed to endorse the check as per the denomination of the principle of Abundance.

Step Seven: Upon completing the check, take a brief moment to visualize the receipt of the funds.

Permit yourself to fully experience the sentiments of gratitude and joy that stem from already possessing the financial resources.

It is crucial to possess the ability to fully immerse oneself in the belief of acquiring this possibility for oneself. . . Indeed, it is true that this occurrence has already transpired within the realm of probability, if nothing else.

Additionally, you may consider employing the technique of mentally envisioning a radiant aura of pure white light enveloping the check, infusing it with revitalizing energy and positively transforming any unfavorable energy or limiting beliefs pertaining to attracting prosperity.

Step Eight: Subsequently, it is permissible to store the check in a designated location or conceal it in an inconspicuous area to avoid unnecessary attention.

Recommended Steps to Take After Completing the Process of Crafting Law of Abundance Manifestation Checks

After composing the check, you have fulfilled your duty by consciously manifesting your desire for enhanced prosperity, henceforth allowing the universe to assume control.

It is crucial to refrain from forming any emotional connections to the outcomes of this exercise. Instead, merely recognize that the influx of money into your life will commence promptly thereafter, and have faith in the Universe's ability to determine the most effortless manner for its manifestation.

The optimal functioning of the Universe is enhanced when it remains undisturbed by your intervention.

Compose a fresh check on a monthly basis, establish novel aspirations, and rest assured that the Universal Genie is dutifully carrying out your commands!

It's all very simple. Please bear in mind that while engaging with abundance checks, it is essential to direct your attention towards the aspects that are presently yielding positive results in your life.

By directing your attention towards experiences that elicit positive emotions, you elevate your vibrational frequency, consequently facilitating the materialization of desired outcomes.

This implies it is crucial to refrain from allocating any time to measurement, scoring, or concerns regarding the manifestation. Instead, it is advised to have faith in the process and relinquish any thoughts that may oppose it.

The objects of our utmost desires are often met with the greatest opposition, hence it is advisable to redirect our attention towards alternative pursuits.

Creating a monetary manifestation request is a method to direct your attention towards your desires and subsequently relinquishing control, enabling the Universe to bestow it upon you.

Put simply, the abundance checks serve as a means to overcome any self-imposed barriers.

Phenomenal vs. Non-Phenomenal

Throughout this chapter, there has been consistent allusion to the notions of phenomenal and non-phenomenal. To provide a brief overview, the term phenomenal pertains to anything that can be directly encountered or perceived. All of the knowledge we possess concerning our world is extraordinary. Anything that extends beyond the realm of human perception can be considered as transcending the phenomenal realm. The cognitive processes within our minds operate in a conceptual manner, whereby incoming information is transformed into abstract constructs.

Verbal and visual representations exemplify the abstract constructs of the human intellect. The manifestation of words and images exclusively stems from the faculties of the human mind. In the absence of cognitive processes, the existence of visual representations and linguistic expressions would be rendered impossible. We are unable to perceive visual representations. As previously indicated, our visual organs perceive visual stimuli, which are subsequently transformed into electrical signals. The brain subsequently transforms the electrical impulses into visual representations. In a similar vein, words can be perceived as cognitive constructs employed to articulate a particular idea. One may be curious as to the reason for my transition in terminology from "mind" to "brain." At this moment, I am employing this choice solely for semantic considerations. We shall further deliberate upon the distinction that exists between the mind and the brain at a later point in time.

Assuming that visual representations are contingent upon the assimilation of data through visual perception, and linguistic expressions serve as cognitive manifestations of thoughts, it begs the question: what are the origins of information and thought? Thought and information are synonymous. The concept we refer to as thought can be understood as information that is apprehended by conscious awareness. At its most essential level, all that exists can be described as information. Nevertheless, we can take an additional stride in that direction. Data constitutes a manifestation of energy. All that exists manifests as various forms of energy. Nevertheless, the energy in question is not of the same nature as the energy we encounter in our everyday existence. The type of energy I am referring to does not pertain to electricity. The energy that I am referring to possesses self-awareness. The phenomenon under discussion pertains to heightened awareness, which is commonly referred to as consciousness.

In the initial segment of this literary work, you engaged in an exercise wherein you conducted an observation of an object. Upon engaging in this exercise, it is anticipated that you have arrived at the realization that the detachment of awareness from an object is, in fact, an unattainable feat. Awareness and consciousness are synonymous, referring to identical concepts. The underlying essence of all existence lies within consciousness. All that which comes into being is derived from the realm of consciousness. Experience is impossible in the absence of consciousness.

Returning to the notions of non-phenomenal and phenomenal, it must be noted that these are mere abstractions employed by the human intellect to elucidate the realm of perceivable and imperceptible phenomena. Indeed, words, concepts, the intellect, this literary work, as well as oneself, represent but the tangible expressions of consciousness. Fundamentally, there exists no discernible distinction between the realm of phenomena and a realm devoid of phenomena. The distinction between spirituality and materialism is nonexistent. There exists an absence of distinction between the realms of reality and fantasy. Ultimately, no distinction can be drawn between your existence and the very essence of the universe. The perception of divergence or uniqueness arises solely from the cognitive faculties of our consciousness.

There exist diligent researchers devoting countless hours to the pursuit of unraveling the origins of the universe or unraveling the nature of matter. Their searches will be perpetual. They are pursuing abstract ideas while the solutions they seek reside within the profound intricacies of their personal experiences.

Daily Exercise:

Please take a seat and grant yourself permission to unwind.

Now, direct your attention to an item that you are acquainted with. Direct your attention towards this object.

After acquainting yourself with this object, proceed to shut your eyes and employ all your mental faculties to envision it as accurately as possible.

Each individual has a unique way of visualizing, therefore refrain from making any assessments regarding your aptitude for visualization. Please endeavor to visualize your object utilizing your utmost capabilities.

Once you have conceptualized the image, take note of the inherent characteristics exhibited by this visualization. What is your perception of this image? Does it exhibit blurriness or clarity? Does it lack discernible characteristics or does it possess vivid details? Do the attributes of your depiction undergo variations in intensity or configuration, or do they endure in a constant manner?

Would you be able to ascertain the origin of the location in which your image materialized? Are you able to ascertain the destination of your image when it experiences fading?

Envision a concept that is purely fictitious, a construct that resides beyond the bounds of your tangible existence. Possibly it could be a mythical creature such as a unicorn or an anomalous entity resembling a purple elephant.

Once the mental image has been formed, take note of the characteristics inherent in this image. What is your perception of this image? Is the image perceived as distorted or sharp? Does it lack distinctive characteristics or is it presented with intricate detail? Do the attributes of your image undergo any alterations in their intensity or form, or do they persist without any significant changes?

Are you able to ascertain the origin of the image in question? Are you capable of ascertaining the destination of your image upon its gradual disappearance?

Is there a disparity between your mental representation of the hypothetical entity and the one that you directly perceived? Are you capable of discerning the distinction between "reality" and "fantasy"?

Exercise Consciousness In All Actions And The Surrounding Context

The majority of individuals struggle to actualize their sincere aspirations, not due to a lack of genuine desire, but rather as a result of being preoccupied with the multitude of disarray in both their personal lives and thoughts. Clutter encompasses any objects, materials, or elements that introduce disorder, disarray, and lack of organization into one's life, thereby diverting attention and hindering the pursuit of genuine objectives. For example, an excessively disorganized desk can hinder your ability to locate essential documents pertaining to a project you are currently engaged in. A mobile device inundated with an excessive influx of messages can impede your capacity to concentrate on the current undertaking.

Likewise, a mind filled with disarray hampers one's ability to concentrate and hinders the effective allocation of one's energy, time, and efforts towards manifesting genuine and profound desires. An excessively disordered and convoluted mind is a dwelling place for pessimistic and purposeless thoughts. Ideas that induce a sense of inadequacy regarding the realization of your objectives, as well as those that divert your attention from your intended purpose, can be classified within this particular realm. When such thoughts occupy your mind, your belief in yourself gradually diminishes, and you begin to cultivate negative and restrictive convictions. These beliefs diminish an individual's overall vibrational frequency, and as you are undoubtedly aware, they bring about a resonance with experiences of a similar nature.

In order to actualize your authentic aspirations, be they tied to the realms of wellness, prosperity, affection, interpersonal connections, contentment, opulence, or spiritual growth, it is imperative to commence the process of eradicating any form of superfluous encumbrance within your existence. This is where exercising self-awareness and being cognizant of one's environment can be advantageous.

By maintaining a heightened sense of self-awareness and attentiveness to one's surroundings, it becomes readily apparent when disorder begins to infiltrate one's existence, prompting prompt measures to eradicate it prior to its escalation and further disarray. To demonstrate and uphold self-awareness, as well as an attentive consideration of one's environment, entails a deliberate cognizance of both internal mental processes and external occurrences.

Despite the belief held by many individuals that they are presently engaged in their lives, the truth is that a significant portion of us dwell in either the past or the future. When one is devoid of self-awareness and fails to fully engage in the tasks at hand, they are likely to exhibit reduced vigilance towards their ruminations and the multitude of undesired occurrences transpiring in their environment. This is precisely the manner in which we inadvertently permit mental and physical disarray to infiltrate our lives.

It holds significant importance to safeguard our minds against any forms of clutter that have the potential to disturb our elevated state of vibration and positive cognitive framework. Let us examine methods for eradication from your daily existence.

De-Clutter Your Life

To eliminate the external disarray, conduct an analysis of your objectives followed by an evaluation of your surroundings and personal circumstances. Compile a comprehensive inventory of all the elements and engagements that are incongruous with your objectives, and commence the process of eliminating them. All documents pertaining to prior endeavors, endeavors undertaken solely for concealed agendas, and individuals who fail to contribute positively to your existence should be eradicated from your existence. It is imperative to selectively retain possessions, individuals, and engagements that truly align with your core values, possess a beneficial impact on your well-being, and contribute to the fulfillment of your objectives. Additionally, it is important to periodically evaluate your surroundings every fortnight to determine if any superfluous items or activities have been incorporated. Engaging in this activity on a Sunday evening prior to the commencement of the work week is highly favorable.

In terms of eliminating your internal clutter, it is advisable to engage in daily mindfulness breathing meditation. It is an uncomplicated yet highly efficacious meditative technique that cultivates self-awareness, enabling one to embrace the present moment and minimize preoccupation with trivial matters. Allow me to provide you with a step-by-step guide on how to effectively engage in this practice.

Please begin by setting a timer for a duration of 2 to 5 minutes and positioning yourself comfortably in a tranquil environment.

Please consider closing your eyes if leaving them open proves to be a source of distraction. Consider recollecting a soothing memory that may assist in inducing a state of relaxation.

Gradually transition your attention from the soothing recollection to your breath, carefully noting the process of inhalation and exhalation as you progressively attain a state of relaxation.

It is customary for individuals who are new to this experience to frequently find themselves daydreaming. When such an occurrence takes place, one should duly recognize its existence, and proceed to gently redirect one's focus towards the act of breathing.

If you are fatigued and feel yourself succumbing to drowsiness, adjust your posture to assume a more upright stance. Please refrain from being disheartened with yourself if your attention deviates due to this or any other cause.

Continuously engage in this activity throughout the entirety of the session, and upon hearing the auditory signal, only commence the act of opening your eyes at your own discretion. Express appreciation to oneself for dedicating time to engage in the practice.

Make it a habit to engage in this practice daily, ideally repeating it at least once or twice. By maintaining this routine consistently, you will observe a progressive enhancement in your level of mindfulness as time goes by. Once you begin cultivating greater self-awareness, it is advisable to gradually extend the duration of your mindfulness practice to encompass intervals of 10, 15, and subsequently 20 minutes, until ultimately achieving the ability to sustain a practice lasting 30 minutes uninterrupted. Over time, you will observe a heightened sense of mindfulness permeating your awareness in every moment.

What will this achieve? The objective of this exercise is to proactively identify any detrimental thoughts prior to their manifestation in your mind, enhance your emotional state, eradicate mental disarray, and refrain from fixating on any adverse aspects of your existence. It aims to facilitate your progress towards your objectives with ease while maintaining elevated levels of vibration.

Step Two: Visualization
Visualization, alternatively known as mental imagery, stands as an immensely influential instrument for programming the subconscious mind. Over the course of numerous decades, a considerable number of accomplished individuals spanning various fields, such as business, entertainment, sports, politics, management, public speaking, and corporate leadership, have harnessed the potential of visualization. This

technique involves the creation of a mental image that represents the desired outcomes they seek to attain, envisioning their success and victorious realization of predetermined objectives. Additionally, there are individuals who employ visualized imagery on multiple occasions throughout the day, harnessing its potential to manifest their profound desires.

Visualization enables you to maintain focus on your desired achievement. Through the power of visualization, one has the potential to transform the negative thoughts regarding one's inability to accomplish a desired objective into an optimistic mindset. This process also enables the elimination of any lingering doubts that may have hindered success in previous attempts to manifest one's desires. By engaging in the practice of envisioning oneself attaining their aspirations, individuals can attain a heightened state of tranquility and imbue themselves with a greater sense of excitement towards the forthcoming endeavors that lie in their path. Visualization is indeed a potent tool to pursue life aspirations, not only due to its capacity to direct attention towards one's potential, but also as it instills motivation and encourages the cessation of self-imposed limitations.

At the onset, the skill of visualization may present challenges, necessitating a period of dedicated effort to fully attain proficiency. An effective approach to visualizing entails envisioning yourself successfully attaining your aspirations. As you may recollect from the preceding section, there was a notable focus on the manner in which it will transpire, rather than solely on its potentiality. Stated differently, you are actively manifesting these dreams and ideas, rather than merely wishing for their fulfillment. Once you have established a comprehensive understanding of your desired course of action and have devised a strategy for its achievement, it is advisable to commence a repetitive iteration of this procedure. Continue this practice until a profound sense of actuality begins to coalesce within the realm of your visualization. This is the manner in which one can materialize these aspirations, by evoking constructive thoughts, optimistic energy, and drawing towards oneself what one puts forth.

Having established a clear mental image, it is now appropriate to commence the implementation of the concrete techniques of visualization. This may encompass the process of mentally picturing objects and visuals, engaging in regulated breathing techniques, and repeating particular affirmative statements. The objective of visualization entails ensuring that your manifested desires align precisely with what you create and attract through the power of visualization.

Please contemplate the activities you aspire to engage in, specifically the moments you desire to experience and the lifestyle you aim to cultivate. Envision yourself having accomplished this objective, and refrain from allowing skepticism to overshadow these thoughts. Consider the perspective of envisioning yourself already possessing it, and contemplate the emotions you would experience upon its attainment. Once you have completed the process of visualizing, make a written record of your desire or goal to enable frequent revisiting. While it may appear trivial, the practice of visualization carries considerable significance. Individuals who engage in frequent visualization often experience a greater level of achievement than anticipated, as they not only conceptualize their goals, as previously explained, but actively manifest them as well.

Elevating Your Frequency

Please consider the occasions in which you experienced a sense of general discomfort or discontent.

You will express that nothing is functioning effectively. You experience instances where your car gets abruptly overtaken or another individual occupies a parking spot that you were anticipating to use.

'Life sucks. It just isn't working'.

The reason for your current condition is that you are not experiencing optimal physical or emotional well-being.

When experiencing a state of discomfort, it is inevitable that one's circumstances will become increasingly unfavorable.

What is feeling?

Feeling is Conscious Awareness. One's emotional state is a direct manifestation of their conscious perception of the vibrational frequency they embody. If one is not experiencing well-being, they are resonating with a negative energy.

Are you aware that it is possible to alter your vibration quite easily?

The physical form in which you currently reside can be described as a molecular arrangement that undergoes rapid vibrational motions.

Everything vibrates; nothing rests. Individuals who are experiencing positive emotions are demonstrating a favorable vibrational state. It is feasible to swiftly align oneself with positive energy.

Music is an exceptional artistic medium for attaining a state of heightened resonance within oneself. Alternative options encompass strolling along the seashore for extended periods, engaging in artistic endeavors such as painting, singing, indulging in comedy performances, or even undertaking an uncomplicated act of reaching out to a cherished acquaintance or family member via telephone.

Music, for instance, serves as an exceptional medium to evoke positive emotions.

If you are exposed to disordered music, you will experience a perturbed vibrational state. If you are playing pleasant, soothing music, it will influence your vibration in a positive manner. Alter your frequency and your disposition will likewise conform. Being in a negative state of mind is not beneficial in any manner. Your level of vibrational frequency determines the quality of your experience. Hence, it is imperative to diligently maintain oneself in a state characterized by optimal vibrations at all times.

Vibration affects even plants, demonstrating their sensitivity. In the presence of disordered energy, the vegetation perishes. When conducted with positive energy, the endeavor flourishes.

Endeavor to cultivate a harmonious ambiance by engaging in activities that induce serenity, such as immersing oneself in melodious compositions, appreciating aesthetically pleasing artworks, partaking in a leisurely moment on a serene shoreline with a beloved literary work, engaging in amiable conversations with companions, and savoring delectable gastronomic delights of personal preference.

Engaging with a motivational recording can likewise cultivate a constructive resonance. Give prominence to cultivating a sense of positive energy in your daily existence.

Make an effort to avoid associating with individuals engaged in negative discussions. The individuals with whom you choose to associate greatly influence the energy you emanate. You should strive to maintain a vigilant state of awareness pertaining to the energy present within your surroundings.

It is of utmost importance that you maintain a highly positive vibrational state. When you are in a positive state of energy, beneficial thoughts effortlessly enter your consciousness. You will witness a more optimal approach to the task at hand.

You will enhance your proficiency in whatever endeavor you pursue, and ultimately, this is the desired outcome. You aspire to achieve exemplary outcomes. There is a current of energy that is perpetually coursing through you, and when it enters your awareness, it assumes a formless state. Our cognitive processes shape its structure, and as we assimilate it. It regulates the bodily oscillation.

Maintain a positive energy in your body, and you will find yourself functioning in accordance with your desires, engaging in activities of your choice.

Maintain a state of elevated resonance by engaging in activities that promote positive energy, such as listening to uplifting music, enriching audio recordings, surrounding yourself with supportive companions, or immersing yourself in stimulating literature.

The Significance of Mindset in Context

It is well-established that all entities, including both our physical and mental aspects, are composed of energy. This signifies that our thoughts possess an energetic nature as well. The power of our thoughts lies in their capacity to generate an intangible force that emanates from the depths of the consciousness. Extensive research has been conducted on this phenomenon, commonly referred to as the concept of Mind Power.

The notion that our mental constructs profoundly impact not only our individual existence but also those in our proximity. Our thoughts have an impact on individuals within our tangible realm. Due to the principle of the law of attraction, all the events that occur in our lives are a result of our own magnetic influence, drawing them towards us.

One prevalent adage often encountered in teachings on the law of attraction is that similar elements have a propensity to be drawn towards one another. It constitutes the foremost principle within the domain of the law of attraction, thus warranting a more comprehensive analysis of its implications for us and the intricate manner in which it permeates our lives.

To commence, I would like to inquire about something. What is your work? What task or obligation do you need to fulfill? There is a collective endeavor that each of us must undertake for the realization of a remarkable existence that we all merit, but it is of a nature divergent from convention. The task at hand does not involve attempting to possess a particular demeanor or eliciting a desired response. Rather, the essential task consists of granting oneself permission to surrender and embrace the tranquil presence of the divine.

It is unnecessary to make efforts to locate this frequency, as it naturally dwells within you. It resides within each and every individual, without any exclusions. There are typical activities that individuals engage in to unwind, such as the practice of meditation and conducting affirmations.

Now, I am about to present you with an unexpected challenge. There is no need for you to seek external sources of attraction, as everything you require already resides within you. We were all brought into existence with the purpose of perceiving our own existence as a means of externalizing elements and incorporating them internally. This is the reason why it is referred to as the law of attraction.

Nevertheless, it is a fact that everything you may desire in life already exists within the depths of your being. It is unnecessary to procure these items externally. If it appears that your deepest desires are not being realized, it is probable that you are unintentionally repelling them through conflicting frequencies.

All phenomena are composed of energy, each possessing a distinctive frequency. Each frequency possesses distinct characteristics, resulting in a perception that everything and everyone appears detached from oneself. Nevertheless, entities are not discrete, and all entities are integral components within the interconnected fabric of energy. When you adjust your frequencies to align with your aspirations, this is when you "draw towards yourself" that which has perpetually existed. Your previously imperceptible inclination has now manifested itself as a result of a shift in frequency. This is the point at which you observe the materialization of it within your tangible reality. The aspiration or vision has been present since the very beginning, but you had been functioning on a distinct wavelength.

Real-Life Examples

It is a simple matter to inform an individual that we are inclined to draw, or become aware of, phenomena that align with our vibrational state. However, it is quite another matter to substantiate this verity in actuality. In order to substantiate the principle of 'like attracts like', let us now examine several authentic anecdotes. This study will examine the concept of the law of attraction through a therapeutic lens. Specifically dysfunctional relationships.

Individuals with prior experience in relationships often possess the capacity to perceive the shortcomings of their partners, yet they frequently struggle to recognize their own contributions to the existing issues. Nonetheless, as a consequence of the principle stating that similar entities are drawn to each other, your ultimate outcome aligns with that of your partner. This is because individuals tend to attract those who share a comparable state of physical wellbeing, emotional distress, and the like.

This implies that the extent to which you opt to disengage emotionally from yourself, by engaging in self-judgment, resorting to addictive behaviors, disregarding your emotions, or attributing responsibility for your emotional state to others, is the same extent to which your partner will likewise disengage emotionally from themselves.

When an individual initiates criticism towards their partner, it is probable that they are reproaching themselves and possibly surrendering their own identity to their partner in hopes of gaining their validation. Both individuals are exerting a certain level of control, although one is conscious solely of the manipulative influence imposed upon them by the other. Suppose Pam asserts that Mark is disengaging, simultaneously conveying her displeasure. It represents contrasting facets of their dysfunctional nature. The matter at hand pertains to the fact that Pam and Mark entered into a relationship with the intention of seeking love, rather than focusing on self-discovery and cultivating self-love before extending that love to one another.

Is this something that you would like to confront? While it is true that similar individuals tend to be drawn to one another, it is crucial to emphasize that this does not imply an obligation to cultivate adversarial connections. By cultivating self-love, one is able to draw towards oneself individuals who possess the ability to reciprocate such affection, thereby fostering a more harmonious and unified bond. Let us now examine the implications of fostering a mutually compatible state of emotional well-being.

To engender an emotional equilibrium that aligns with your prevailing state of well-being necessitates undertaking personal growth and healing endeavors aimed at mitigating insecurities and dispelling feelings of shame. This implies that you possess the knowledge of cultivating self-love and subsequently extending that same love towards others. This entails the cessation of self-neglect and the acquisition of self-compassion, signifying a recognition of personal accountability for one's emotions. It involves turning away from evading or attributing one's feelings to external influences.

After gaining the knowledge of self-worth and assuming accountability for your own emotions, it is unlikely that you will be able to attract an individual who consistently neglects their own emotional needs. Consequently, you will attract individuals who have a strong sense of self-worth and prioritize the act of giving love rather than receiving it. Consequently, you will not be paired with an individual who engages in judgmental behavior, withdraws emotionally, assigns blame, or adopts a victim mentality. You will not experience an attraction towards this individual due to their lack of alignment with the commonly accepted standards of emotional well-being.

It is understood that all things resonate at disparate frequencies. Individuals who exhibit a low frequency are those who engage in self-neglect and experience feelings of insecurity. They will appeal to individuals who resonate at the same lower frequency. Individuals with an elevated vibrational state are those who prioritize and have a profound appreciation for their own well-being, thereby drawing in like-minded individuals. Individuals who exhibit qualities of self-compassion, compassion towards others, generosity, emotional stability, openness, and positivity will not experience an inclination towards individuals who seek excessive attention and approval, embrace negativity, and maintain a closed mindset.

Although individuals generally do not actively seek out individuals who display neediness, negativity, and closed-mindedness, it is highly likely that these are the types of individuals one will inadvertently attract into their life if they possess such qualities. In order to cultivate a functional and affectionate relationship, it is imperative to invest effort in acquiring the skills of emotional accountability. This will mean:

Acquiring the ability to engage in self-care rather than relying on others to fulfill that need.

Acquiring the ability to discover an inner wellspring of spiritual love, rather than relying on external individuals to assume the role of a higher authority.

Remaining receptive to gaining further understanding about your emotions rather than safeguarding oneself against them via self-criticism and dependencies.

Acquiring the skill of being fully engaged in the physical realm rather than being confined within the confines of one's thoughts and attempting to evade emotional experiences.

This concept is applicable to various facets of your life, as cultivating self-love has the potential to elevate your vibrational frequency in all aspects of your existence.

In Your Daily Endeavors, Embody The Persona That You Have Envisioned For Yourself.

Upon envisioning your future self or future reality, it becomes unmistakably evident that a transformation of your character is imperative. Many of the worries, anxieties, and apprehensions that you experience on a daily basis at present will vary once you attain that particular condition. As you engage in visualization, you promptly discern the mental state you would inhabit in that scenario.

For instance, envision yourself possessing a net worth of ten billion dollars. In addition to envisioning oneself residing in alternative locations, possessing a range of possessions, engaging with individuals from various backgrounds, and frequenting multiple destinations, one would observe a notable transformation in their personality. Your perspective would be altered. Your perception, in this context, is serving to enlighten you.

In order to genuinely envisage this reality, it is imperative that you first embody the persona that you aspire to project. It is excessively simplistic to solely fixate on the extravagant automobiles, substantial wealth, immense professional acclaim, and similar factors. These are the outcomes derived from a more substantial source. It is possible to achieve those accomplishments due to the fact that you have undergone personal transformation or experienced a shift in cognitive processes. The primary objective of visualization is to intricately dissect and immerse oneself into the mindset of the individual one aspires to become. This individual is the one who has attained this ultimate reality.

Acquire insight into the cognitive processes of that individual. Presently, this circumstance transcends mere fantasization of assuming a different physical form or merely assessing the necessary acquisition of emotional aptitudes. While acknowledging the significance of those aspects, it is imperative to engage in a more pragmatic course of action. In your everyday existence, assume the persona of that individual—behave as though you have already become him. What holds significance in his eyes? What is his perspective on the world?

Begin perceiving the world in a similar manner. Behave in a manner consistent with the assumption of possessing a net worth of one billion dollars. It is imperative for you to comprehend that the primary factor contributing to your sense of constraint, disillusionment, and difficulty is minimally attributable to your material possessions. Should you require verification, it is worth noting that a substantial proportion of individuals of limited financial means who emerge as lottery winners eventually find themselves in a state of destitution once more within a span of a few years. They file for bankruptcy and revert to their prior patterns, subsequently experiencing a recurrence of financial difficulties.

Irrespective of the magnitude of the monetary sums they handled. From their perspective, it is akin to $H2O$. Today it's here. Tomorrow it's gone. They have reverted back to a state of extreme dryness. Conversely, certain individuals with vast wealth occasionally make unfavorable business choices. They terminate business operations and file for insolvency. Nevertheless, these individuals never face financial insolvency due to their ability to establish another enterprise and persistently make attempts. Prior to their awareness, they find themselves in an improved circumstance.

The absence of monetary resources does not inherently cause unhappiness, just as the possession of wealth does not inherently confer richness upon an individual. It transcends that—it is a matter of one's perspective. Regrettably, individuals of misfortune solely perceive deprivation and insufficiency, directing their attention towards the absence of elements. Many individuals are motivated by their apprehension of deprivation or the prospect of being left in a disadvantaged position.

In numerous instances, a considerable segment of individuals grappling with poverty would prioritize proactive actions or undertake calculated risks solely when they perceive an overwhelming sense of urgency or constraint. Until that juncture, they would persist in their ongoing activities. That is a valid point, however, one must bear the consequences of their actions.

In contrast, affluent individuals display a lower aversion to risk. They strategically undertake calculated risks and reap substantial rewards. This situation represents actuality, where greater risk corresponds to greater reward.

It is not the tangible wealth that distinguishes the affluent from the disadvantaged. It's the mindset. When one envisages the alternative reality one aspires for, as epitomized by their ultimate objectives, it becomes imperative to examine their mindset at that juncture.

How might an individual of such remarkable accomplishment perceive their life, assess the path ahead of them, and formulate choices? By consistently and deliberately embodying the traits and behaviors of that individual on a daily basis, you enhance the pace at which your aspirations materialize. There exists a traditional aphorism which states, "In order to amass one million dollars, one must present oneself in a manner suggestive of opulence."

That's partially true. Indeed, when individuals consistently interact with you in a particular manner, it inevitably influences your perceptions of self and subsequently impacts your behavioral responses in alignment with their anticipated standards. One can elicit this response from others by donning the attire of someone they aspire to emulate. The sole element that is absent is the mentality.

There exists an alternative approach for accomplishing this task. Furthermore, in addition to adorning oneself in attire befitting a substantial fortune, one may also adopt a mindset akin to that of an individual already in possession of a significant sum of one million dollars. Behave as though you possess the wealth of a billionaire. When engaging in this activity, you are consistently honing your skills through repetitive practice. You are practicing your verbal interactions with others. You are proactively strategizing the courses of action you will pursue upon the emergence of opportunities. Above all, you are actively shaping the vibrations you emit to the cosmos, which adhere steadfastly to a distinct frequency, thereby establishing a profound connection to your overarching aspirations.

According to the traditional adage, repetition leads to permanence. Thus, when one consistently engages in the process of envisioning and permitting oneself to be emotionally captivated by said vision, one begins to manifest these emotions in their daily actions. In due time, your assumptions and expectations in the present moment become influenced by the regular visualization choices you make.

Strategies For Actualizing Abundance And Attaining Economic Empowerment

Have you grown weary of embracing the monotonous and competitive nature of modern life? Are you weary of consistently allocating your finances towards debt repayment? Are you interested in cultivating greater financial abundance in your life? Are you interested in leading a life characterized by opulence and extravagance?

There was a time when each of us harbored aspirations for wealth or, at the very least, a more affluent existence. Fortunately, it is within your capacity to employ the universally recognized principle of attraction in order to draw greater prosperity into your existence. The universal law of attraction can be utilized to manifest the long-desired state of financial liberation.

Presented below are the sequential guidelines that elucidate the utilization of the law of attraction as a means to bring about affluence and liberation from financial constraints in one's existence:

Express your intention to have more money by writing it down. Kindly refrain from composing statements such as "I aspire to attain wealth." It is imperative for you to provide explicit details. Please specify the desired amount of funds and provide a deadline for manifestation to the universe. Compose a statement along the lines of, "My aspiration is to amass a sum of $1 million within a span of two years." It is crucial to bear in mind that your objective should align with your personal preferences and comfort level. It is imperative that you maintain a belief in the feasibility of attaining your objective.

Refrain from entertaining pessimistic thoughts regarding finances. The majority of individuals have been ingrained with the belief that money possesses negative connotations, and that only individuals engaged in dishonest practices attain wealth. In order to attain affluence, it is imperative to cultivate a sense of ease and familiarity with financial matters. Astoundingly, a notable portion of individuals express their desire for wealth, while simultaneously harboring unease towards the prospect of possessing substantial monetary resources due to their accustomed circumstances of poverty. Of greater significance, refrain from pondering one's financial obligations. Numerous authorities in the realm of the law of

111

attraction maintain that opting to configure automatic payments for all one's obligations and debts is a highly recommended approach, as it obviates the need for monthly concerns and anxieties pertaining to them.

Envision yourself in possession of significant wealth. Envision the quality of life that awaits you once you attain the financial means you have long aspired for. What purchases do you intend to make with the entirety of your financial resources? What is the sensation of residing in a tremendously opulent lifestyle? What is your experience like when operating your high-end vehicle? What is the experience of residing in a spacious residence like? What is the sensation you experience when beholding a substantial balance in your checking account? Contemplate the prospect of allocating additional funds, and envision the sensations associated with significant expenditure. It is essential to thoroughly visualize each aspect, as the universe holds a preference for meticulous attention to detail. It is imperative to construct the desired life within the realm of one's thoughts, as it is in this conceptualization that the manifestation of such a reality can be achieved in the tangible realm.

Recite the subsequent declarations with unwavering certainty on a daily basis:

I am leading a life of considerable comfort.
I am wealthy.
I exclusively harbor favorable sentiments towards affluence.
On a daily basis, my financial resources increase.

Acquiring and managing substantial financial resources has become inherent to my being.

I express my gratitude for the abundance of financial resources that I possess.

I am strongly drawn to wealth, and conversely, wealth is inexplicably drawn to me.

I am receptive to acquiring additional financial assets.

I am receptive to opportunities that will enhance my financial assets and expand my wealth.

I acquire my wealth through honorable means.

I derive pleasure from my affluence and have a deep appreciation for the generation of wealth.

I derive pleasure from the process of acquiring wealth.

I derive immense satisfaction from the complete journey of accumulating wealth and increasing monetary resources.

In order to enhance the influx of wealth into your life, it is imperative to demonstrate gratitude for all that you possess. Expressing gratitude will attract an amplified abundance of experiences and cultivate an enduring sense of satisfaction and joy. When one expresses gratitude for one's current possessions, one tends to draw more of those possessions into one's life.

Initiate decisive measures and carefully strategize your path to attain triumph. Despite the potency of the law of attraction, its efficacy will remain dormant unless accompanied by your proactive participation. The principle of attraction holds the potential to present you with lucrative prospects, however, it is imperative that you actively engage and fulfill your responsibilities. Perform your duties with utmost proficiency to increase your chances of career advancement, resulting in enhanced financial remuneration. To attain success as an entrepreneur, it is advised to actively seek out suitable avenues for business expansion, along with potential investors. If your aspiration is to pursue a career in education, I recommend considering the option of undertaking the qualifying examination. If you have aspirations to explore different parts of the globe, I recommend initiating your search for favorable offers on airfare and lodging.

Exemplary Guidelines For Optimal Health And Interpersonal Connections

Are you familiar with the tale of King Midas? If that is not the case, allow me to elucidate: in ancient Greece, there resided a renowned monarch by the name of Midas. One day, the Divine Deity appeared to him in a dream and requested the granting of a desired divine favor. After extensive contemplation, he proceeded to make a request: that any object with which he makes contact undergoes a transformation, turning into the precious metal, gold. The deity granted his desire, and upon awakening the following day, he endeavored to test the bestowed blessing. He made contact with various objects such as a water fountain, trees, flowers, and butterflies, and observed a remarkable transformation as these items were all transmuted into gold. He was truly captivated by the blessing and derived pleasure from the act of transforming everything into Gold through tactile contact. Ultimately, he experienced a sensation of hunger and proceeded to request sustenance in the form of nourishment and refreshment. However, to his dismay, even the provision of food and water transformed into solid gold. Afterwards, when his cherished daughter approached him and he desired to embrace her, she too underwent a transformation, becoming gold. He wept profusely, and thereafter, a divine manifestation occurred, whereupon he beseeched the Almighty to retract the bestowed favor. Hence, we may extrapolate from this narrative that prior to aspiring for wealth and influence, it is imperative to prioritize our existing assets, specifically our well-being and interpersonal connections.

Our good health is truly one of the most valuable blessings bestowed upon us by the divine being. Upon perusing the renowned literary work titled "The Monk Who Sold his Ferrari," I came to the realization that a notable litigator, who had been immersed in the relentless pursuit of wealth and material possessions, suffered a cardiac event. Subsequently, he became cognizant of the inherent peril his health was subjected to amidst this ceaseless pursuit. He divested himself of all his material possessions and embarked on a quest to discover the means to maintain his physical well-being and energy. During his expedition, he encountered numerous monks from whom he acquired knowledge on maintaining physical and mental well-being, while embracing existence to its utmost potential. Therefore, I recommend that you carefully consider the resources currently at your disposal. Maintaining good health is essential in order to fully appreciate and benefit from the material aspects of life, and it is important to prioritize your well-being in order to cultivate a healthy body and mind that can support your positive aspirations in life.

Your interpersonal connections hold significant value within the realm of your existence. In today's society, there is a noticeable trend towards individuals adopting a materialistic mindset and disregarding empathy, leading them to assess their worth solely based on financial wealth and social standing. In contemporary society, it is becoming increasingly common to observe both young men and women engaging in romantic relationships primarily driven by financial gain, where material wealth and resources play a substantial role. Numerous young women of contemporary society express contentment in participating in a casual encounter for the sake of enjoying some libations, embarking on a scenic excursion, and receiving an exquisite gesture of generosity. In contemporary times, human relationships have increasingly transformed into commodified entities with a disposable nature. One enters into matrimony with an individual primarily motivated by their social status, influence, wealth, and assets, only to terminate the union by means of a divorce agreement when one grows disinterested. I do not recommend adopting such a lifestyle. Your spouse is akin to your true companion, and it is essential to exercise discernment when selecting them, basing your choice on qualities beyond mere wealth and social standing. While it is important to consider financial compatibility when entering into a partnership, I would not recommend marrying someone solely for their wealth. Your interpersonal connections also wield significant influence in cultivating both your mental and physical well-being for a life characterized by health and prosperity.

Envision having a supportive spouse who does not place excessive emphasis on material wealth. In the evening, you engage in intimate conversation with her on the bed, during which she imparts uplifting reflections on your life and its outcomes. You retire to sleep with a positive mindset, and upon waking the next day, you remain in possession of that same positive mindset as you proceed to the workplace. By adopting this approach, you will experience a significant enhancement in the ease with which you live your life, allowing for a heightened capacity to cultivate positive aspirations.

However, should you find yourself married to an individual who possesses no genuine concern for your well-being, but rather, is solely focused on your financial resources, it is likely that disputes would arise regularly, leading to a perpetual state of discord. Consequently, this unfavorable mindset would become firmly rooted within your subconscious. In this instance, you would encounter numerous challenges when endeavoring to cultivate a mindset primed for optimistic aspirations. Therefore, exercise prudence when selecting your associations in order to cultivate a mindset conducive to positive aspirations.

Yoga & Manifestation
Implementing physical exertions to enhance receptivity and alignment with the laws of attraction.

A typical yoga session has a duration of approximately one hour. However, upon reaching the conclusion of this time period, one will enter a state known as Shoonya, characterized by a profound sense of nothingness. In this state, the practitioner will encounter reality as an impartial observer. The outcomes that are envisioned and presented to the observer during this period will materialize in their actuality. Hence, the procedure commences with the sun salutation, also known as "Soorya namaskar." It is imperative to perform these postures with utmost composure. Consider yourself to be akin to a flowing substance. Embody the postures you assume. Instill a subtle degree of tension, while ensuring that neither the practitioner nor the pose itself becomes fatigued. Practicing these postures enhances your fluidity akin to consciousness. Concentrate and maintain awareness of each and every pose you assume. It is imperative to access the state of flow. Once you have achieved a state of flow, you will be reluctant to cease your efforts, and as you witness the transformative power of your visualizations becoming reality, you will continue diligently practicing these poses each and every morning.

Please keep in mind that it is important to limit your exertion to a level that is within your body's capabilities. Excessive efforts may impede the efficacy of the exercise in achieving the desired outcomes. As previously mentioned, adherence to the following three fundamental principles is imperative prior to engaging in any yogic practice:

Digestive tracts must be clean and empty.

Impeccable cleanliness is essential.

Light and loose cloths.

Please adhere to the sequence of postures depicted in the diagram in the correct succession. This chapter will guide you through a series of exercises. Please swiftly navigate through this chapter and proceed to the subsequent chapter. You can follow the exercises mentioned in this chapter the next morning. The optimal timing for accomplishing these tasks while ensuring adherence to all three of these regulations would be during the morning hours. If you find it challenging to memorize or execute these poses through the book, there are numerous instructional videos available on YouTube that you can watch while performing them. Keep in mind that it is imperative to execute all of these actions with utmost grace and serenity. Each repetition of every pose should ideally last for approximately 25 to 45 seconds, and possibly even longer. You have the option to perform 3 to 9 repetitions of this exercise before progressing to the next activity, with 9 repetitions being the recommended ideal range. Following the completion of each exercise, it is imperative that you recline and take a momentary pause for one to two minutes before proceeding to the subsequent exercise. This activity is not intended for physical exertion, therefore it is advised against attempting to reduce body fat through its execution. The initial depiction encompasses the initial series of exercises.

The aforementioned exercise is referred to as sun salutation. Upon finishing the aforementioned exercise, move on to the cobra pose, also known as "Bhujangasana," as depicted in the image displayed on the following page.

Please perform several repetitions of this exercise. Maintain a consistent and unhurried pace, allowing yourself to keep your eyes shut in order to keenly observe your actions and enhance your awareness of them. This sequence of movements is succeeded by the half locust and full locust poses. Below, the depiction of a semi-locust is presented. To maintain proper form, it is recommended to refrain from exhaling while raising your legs. Complete this exercise using both legs and then progress to the full locust posture.

Full locust pose entails elevating both legs and holding the position for a duration of 9-12 seconds per repetition. Two repetitions of the full locust exercise would suffice. The illustration below depicts the complete locust pose.

Upon completing these two postures, namely a mildly challenging pose and an alternative one known as Bow pose (also referred to as "Dhanurasana"). Should you possess the confidence in your abilities, I encourage you to proceed and attempt the task. If one experiences discomfort during the execution of this task, it is imperative to promptly discontinue and proceed to the subsequent one. In this scenario, we shall assume a posture resembling that of a bow, with our arms assuming the role of a taut string maintaining the bow's structural integrity. The position is depicted as depicted below. This pose can be maintained for a duration of 6 to 12 seconds per repetition. 1-2 reps in total.

After the completion of all these tasks. You have completed the second set of exercises. The bow pose presents a slightly greater level of difficulty compared to the other poses, therefore I recommend that you take a brief period of rest. The second set comprised of postures involving spinal movements in a posterior direction.

Moving forward, the forthcoming set will encompass poses focused on spinal extension. Let us commence with the asana commonly known as "Janushirasana" denoting the posture of bringing the head towards the knee. Please maintain this position for a duration of 12 to 15 seconds. Perform one to two repetitions for each leg.

After completing the task, proceed to replicate the action with both legs extended in a forward-facing position. This particular posture is referred to as "Pashchimotanasana".

Once this pose has been completed, take a moment to relax. The imperative to unwind following each posture is imperative, as it enables you to execute subsequent poses in a state of calmness. Afterward, we shall proceed to perform the shoulder stand pose, as illustrated in the subsequent statement.

The shoulder stand pose can pose difficulties for certain individuals. Nevertheless, individuals of a younger age can effortlessly accomplish this task! In this scenario, one must utilize the assistance of their elbows to maintain a state of erectness. You have the option to engage in this activity for a duration of 1 minute or extend it to as long as 5 minutes, should you so desire. Kindly be mindful to refrain from ingesting during the posture. If you believe that you are incapable of performing this pose, it is acceptable. You may proceed to the subsequent task. Prioritizing safety above all else, followed by gradual progression. Engaging in a comprehensive range of poses will ultimately lead to attaining the state of Shoonya, as the body has already been energized through the initial set of poses. These are just reinforcements.

According to specific data, the number of individuals engaging in daily meditation has demonstrated a noticeable growth trend over the years. It is anticipated that this positive trajectory will persist, inspiring a further surge in participation. There remains a significant portion of the population who abstain from engaging in the practice of meditation, and it is my earnest desire to impel and advocate for the widespread adoption of this beneficial practice among individuals. One may question, "What is the rationale behind practicing meditation?" Allow me to elaborate that meditation is utterly costless. It is very powerful. This activity can be performed in any place, promoting feelings of happiness and offering numerous advantages. Let us take a step back and ascertain the precise nature of meditation.

The practice of meditation dates back to antiquity and possesses the capacity to cultivate mental mastery, enabling individuals to explore their inner selves and exercise agency over their own lives. I personally employ it as a means to pacify my thoughts and rejuvenate my energy reserves. Have you experienced such a situation? Your cognition has been wholly commandeered, rendering it difficult to extricate particular thoughts from its grasp. You are devoid of any vigor and are excessively fatigued to the point where even sleep evades you. Meditation has the inherent ability to improve your overall well-being, enabling you to lead a life characterized by utmost joy and contentment. Meditation facilitates the alleviation of anxiety, concerns, pessimistic ideations, and any obstacles that may hinder one's experience of contentment. Extensive evidence supports the notion that engaging in consistent meditation practices effectively alleviates anxiety and stress-related symptoms.

By establishing a consistent practice of meditation, you will experience notable improvements in your mental well-being and develop enhanced resilience in dealing with challenging circumstances. One does not necessitate a conversion to Hinduism or Buddhism in order to engage in meditation, as meditation itself is independent of religious affiliation. You don't even have to sit for hours in the lotus position.

The majority of individuals require a rationale to engage in any activity. In the event that one's physical well-being is compromised, there is a heightened inclination to explore alternative approaches aimed at achieving better health, including the practice of meditation. There is no requirement for you to have a justification for commencing your meditation practice. Despite one's contentment with their life, meditation can still prove beneficial. It possesses the potential to enhance one's quality of life and serves as a preventative measure against various health complications.

Presently, we have become accustomed to expedient remedies. Everywhere you look, you will see all kinds of advertisements that promise you that in just a short time you will feel better without having to do one thing. I am referring to conditions such as anxiety, sleep disturbances, migraines, and various other health ailments that do not necessarily require pharmaceutical intervention. One must acquire the knowledge and skill of practicing meditation.

Meditation encompasses a multitude of advantageous outcomes, which have been rigorously substantiated through scientific inquiry.

Health Benefits:

Recharge your batteries

Delays the aging process

Enhances the strength of the immune system.

Lowers blood pressure

Protects against stress

Gets rid of problems caused by tension

Decreases tension

Psychological Benefits:

Facilitates personal growth Promotes personal development Aids in personal advancement Contributes to personal progress

More confidence

More clarity

Eliminates concerns

Provides increased levels of energy

Controls anger

Facilitates the development of increased sensitivity and tolerance.

Comforts

Soothes

Calms

Work Benefits:

Facilitates the cultivation of creativity

Aids in attaining a sense of command in the face of a tumultuous circumstance.

Learn easier

More receptive

Better memory

Eliminates disturbances.

Helps concentration

It is truly remarkable to comprehend the multitude of advantages one can obtain by engaging in serene introspection through the act of meditation, wherein one remains still and refrains from any activity.

Simple Tips

It is of utmost importance that no one interrupts your meditation practice. It is imperative that you switch off your mobile device, securely shut the door to your present location, and communicate to all individuals that your undisturbed state is required. This is your time.

The room or location in which you are present should not possess an excessive level of luminosity. Ensure that you are dressed in comfortable attire. It is imperative that the environment designated for your meditation endeavors should provide a sense of comfort and satisfaction. In the event of a confined atmosphere, it is recommended to ventilate the area by opening a window, and the utilization of incense has been shown to be beneficial. It is advisable to refrain from engaging in meditation immediately following a meal. Select a time when your energy level is not particularly high. It is advised to abstain from consuming any caffeine prior to engaging in meditation. Endeavor to engage in daily meditation at a consistent hour. This will facilitate the establishment of a new habit.

Similar to any other acquired skill in your personal journey, mastering the art of meditation will necessitate a considerable investment of time and effort to ensure its proper execution. The greater amount of practice you engage in, the swifter your learning will occur, resulting in an increased array of advantages. During the practice of meditation, it is common for thoughts to enter the mind. There is no need for you to become frustrated or anxious. It is imperative to recognize and accept these thoughts, while persevering with the practice of meditation. Engaging in closed-eye meditation can pose challenges for individuals who are new to the practice. Consider engaging in a contemplative practice using a lit candle. By illuminating a candle and employing it as a central point, you can enhance and fortify your focus. This approach proves to be highly efficacious. What is the methodology you employ to accomplish this? Assume a comfortable seated posture and position a lit candle at eye level, ensuring that the flame is just beginning to kindle. After directing your gaze towards the flame for an extended duration, proceed to close your eyes and conjure a mental image of the aforementioned flame. Please endeavor to sustain this position for the maximum duration possible. Through diligent practice, you will notice a progressive increase in the duration of visibility of the flame. There is no obligation for you to assume a crossed leg position. One may engage in meditation in the usual seated position or opt to recline. If you opt to recline, it is advised against meditating while having a candle present. If it is agreeable to you, you may assume a seated position with your legs crossed.

The primary concern lies in ensuring that you experience a sense of comfort and refrain from striving for perfection.

Commence by allocating five minutes to this activity daily, gradually augmenting the duration as per your capacity. Each individual's journey will vary, and it may require patience before any noticeable outcomes become apparent.

This is completely normal. If one were to enroll at a fitness center, it would be unreasonable to anticipate achieving a well-sculpted physique within a brief span of a few weeks. The greater your efforts, the more expeditiously you shall witness outcomes. The crucial aspect lies in developing a routine. Once the advantages become evident, it will be challenging for you to cease.

The predominant justification individuals offer for not engaging in meditation is: "Regrettably, my schedule does not permit me to allocate time for meditation due to the myriad of responsibilities demanding my attention."

This is yet another justification that we employ. It is imperative that we acquire the ability to prioritize our tasks. To me, the practice of meditation carries equal significance as engaging in essential bodily functions such as using the restroom, slumber, hydration, and nourishment. Regardless of the presence or absence of time, these activities hold significance in our lives.

Engaging in meditative practices can contribute to a heightened sense of self-worth and inner wellbeing. If you are able to fully prioritize the practice of meditation in your mind, it is imperative that you allocate sufficient time to engage in this activity. It is paramount to consistently keep it at the forefront of your thoughts. If you hold a genuine conviction in the practice of meditation, it is imperative to incorporate it as an integral aspect of your daily existence. Engaging in a meditation practice, whether undertaken in the morning or prior to retiring for the night, can undeniably yield profound transformations in one's life.

Optimal Approach To Engage In A Comprehensive Fast

This information is primarily intended for individuals who are new to fasting or those seeking guidance on the proper and safe implementation of fasting practices to protect their well-being. This particular fasting method entails the consumption of solely liquids, such as water or juice exclusively. There is no requirement for you to consume any solid food. This document shall act as a reference for your guidance, outlining the subsequent steps in the process.

STEP 1:

PRIOR TO EXECUTING THE FAST

It is imperative that you formulate a schedule to determine the duration of your intended endeavor. I have engaged in this activity for a duration of three consecutive days, and with the assistance of divine intervention, it is conceivable for you to surpass this accomplishment by further extending the duration. However, it is also advisable to seek medical consultation if you acknowledge any limitations within your bodily functions. As he possesses profound knowledge in offering suitable counsel, tailored to your individual circumstances and desired outcomes from a divine intervention, the duration of this practice may vary. Some have adhered to it diligently for a fortnight, while others have extended it to an entire lunar cycle. Nonetheless, it is indeed viable, yet I still recommend that you remain receptive to the guidance of your inner being. One week prior to the commencement of fasting, it is advisable to gradually reduce food consumption and limit the intake of solid edibles.

Consume a greater quantity of vegetables in order to adequately prepare your body for the upcoming fasting period. Subsequently, commence hydrating yourself adequately to familiarize yourself with the functionality prior to the aforementioned day.

STEP 2

DURING THE PERIOD OF ABSTAINING

This is the opportune occasion during which you are required to allocate an extended portion of the time ordinarily designated for ingestion of meals towards engaging in devout prayer and cultivating moments of serenity with the divine, actively pursuing spiritual connection and faithfully documenting each revelation bestowed by the

Almighty through dreams or visions. To accomplish this, it is imperative that you have a journal or book readily available, accompanied by a pen. These revelations will function as a compass for all of your petitions, as they represent God's communication with you, offering guidance towards the path of success as Psalm 32:8 affirms - "I will instruct and teach you in the way you should go; I will counsel you with my loving eye on you."

Consume ample amounts of water or various types of juices to enhance bodily functions and safeguard against dehydration.

It is imperative to ensure that you retire to bed early, as the initial stage of the fasting period can be quite demanding until the body acclimates and becomes accustomed to the novel regimen.

STEP 3

Upon the conclusion of the fasting period

There is no need to abruptly terminate the duration of fasting; initiating and concluding a fast both entail gradual processes.

Upon reaching the final stages, begin incorporating fruits into your diet gradually, allowing your body to readjust to solid food. Fruits are particularly suitable in this context as they possess a gentle texture and are easily digested by the body. Subsequently, introduce vegetables and liquids into your consumption as well. Make an effort to sustain this rhythm until your body successfully acclimates to its customary mode of functioning. Consuming solid food with a high level of intensity may pose potential harm or disruption to your physiological equilibrium, as your system has not yet fully adapted to its regular functioning. It is therefore advisable to initiate the reintroduction of solid foods through a gradual approach, initially incorporating fruits into your diet to gently reawaken your system before introducing other solid food items.

How To Maximize The Benefits Of These Affirmations

The declarations that you have perused possess remarkable potency. Not only are they potent due to their content, but they also exhibit strength by virtue of being scientifically validated.

However, in order to fully harness the potential of the potent affirmations, it is imperative to emphasize the need for repetition.

With increased repetition, one will find it increasingly effortless to assimilate these concepts into their subconscious. Moreover, through the consistent repetition of these affirmations, you will emit the appropriate signals to the cosmos, thus forming a formidable alliance with the universe and effectively enlisting its support.

Additionally, there is a favorable impact that arises from altering one's vibrational frequency. If one possesses knowledge of vibrational principles, it is evident that engaging in higher frequency vibrations is conducive to manifesting positive outcomes in one's life. Furthermore, are you aware of a particularly straightforward method to attain a heightened vibrational frequency? Indeed, the purpose is to reiterate constructive messages, and that is precisely the outcome one can expect from practicing these affirmations. This, in essence, represents the fundamental mechanics behind the process of manifestation, and through the consistent iteration of these potent affirmations, you will actively engage the governing principles of universal manifestation. By doing so, you will harness the manifestation capabilities of the cosmos and attract an abundance of positive occurrences into your life.

These potent affirmations possess the capability to engender a positive influence on your life, regardless of being perused merely once daily. However, as you increase the frequency of their recitation, their potential to affect your life in a positive manner proportionally amplifies.

To further enhance their effectiveness, one can recite them in front of a mirror. I cannot explain the reason behind it, but there seems to be a heightened propensity for one's mind to assimilate these affirmations into their intrinsic programming when they consciously utter them while maintaining direct eye contact with themselves. Perhaps there is a cognitive-spiritual correlation occurring in that instance. I lack a precise scientific explanation for this phenomenon; however, I can confidently assert that engaging in this practice notably enhanced the efficacy of the affirmations I employed. It is a personal suggestion; feel free to utilize it at your discretion.

The level of emotional investment you dedicate to these affirmations when uttering them also influences their efficacy. It is a widely accepted fact that everything in existence possesses an energetic nature. In light of this understanding, it is imperative to imbue these affirmations with a substantial amount of emotional intensity, as it will undoubtedly enhance their energetic potency. Consequently, it will enhance their overall efficiency. The degree of effectiveness of these affirmations will increase proportionally as you amplify the levels of emotion and feeling expressed while vocalizing them. By imbuing these affirmations with fervor, sentiment, and constructive vigor, you will facilitate an enhanced receptiveness of your mind towards them. Occasionally, individuals may experience an unusual sensation while reciting an affirmation. The process of overcoming that sensation becomes more manageable when you incorporate a sense of emotion and vitality into your affirmations. Therefore, articulate them with assurance and utter them with conviction, displaying unwavering belief (even if such belief may not initially be genuine; adopt the strategy of feigning confidence until it becomes a reality).

Additionally, I would like to emphasize the importance of engaging in the practice of documenting these affirmations. This practice possesses a robust scientific foundation, as research pertinently demonstrates that the act of putting pen to paper improves our ability to effectively retain information. Furthermore, documenting information also facilitates the assimilation of ideas by our subconscious cognition. Therefore, in order to enhance the potency and efficacy of your practice, it is advisable to transcribe these affirmations. I am currently in the midst of developing a daily diary to aid in addressing these matters. Therefore, I encourage you to anticipate its release should it pique your interest.

In conclusion, optimal utilization of these potent affirmations can be achieved through the following methods:

Repeating them

Uttering those words in the presence of a reflective surface

Expressing them assertively and with conviction

Writing them

Reiterating them further.

The efficacy of repetition is truly indescribable and cannot be emphasized sufficiently. The greater the frequency with which you recite these affirmations, the more profound their influence will become. Furthermore, increasing the frequency of this practice will facilitate the expeditious integration of these affirmations into your subconscious mind. Consequently, your subconscious will generate novel internal instructions and initiatives in order to manifest favorable outcomes.

Furthermore, as you continue to practice and reiterate these concepts, you will find that they gradually transition into becoming ingrained in your thinking and behaviors. Through the act of repetition (and executing it proficiently by implementing the aforementioned strategies), you will ultimately establish self-fulfilling prophecies.

Affirmations possess significant potency, and this collection of thirty affirmations undoubtedly represents some of the most formidable statements I have encountered or crafted. I devoted numerous years to crafting these, and they represent the culmination of my personal journey's obstacles and achievements. I sincerely aspire that they will yield an equally transformative influence on your life, akin to the profound impact they have borne on mine. Indeed, it is firmly believed that these affirmations will yield a positive influence in your life, but their efficacy hinges solely upon your unwavering commitment to diligently incorporate them into your daily routine and consistently recite them.

It takes a bit of work, practicing these affirmations, but the results totally make the small amount of work that it takes worth the effort, won't you agree?

Chapter Four - Maintain Belief

The possession of unwavering faith is recognized as a crucial factor in the process of manifestation. Numerous individuals have endeavored to utilize the principle of the law of attraction, yet have been unsuccessful in materializing their desired outcomes due to harboring inherent doubts within themselves. They display a lack of patience and are prone to becoming easily disheartened if their desires are not fulfilled within a few months or years.

If one intends to materialize their desired outcomes in life, it is imperative to have unwavering faith in the support and alignment of the universe. It is imperative to maintain optimism and confidence, even in circumstances where current probabilities appear unfavourable. It is imperative that you maintain unwavering faith in the universe's ability to eventually fulfill your desires.

To materialize your aspirations and preferences into tangible reality, it is imperative to cultivate a state of relaxed composure. Numerous metaphysical authorities contend that individuals who possess unwavering faith are often recipients of positive outcomes. Individuals who possess certainty regarding the final result are capable of patiently awaiting it without any sense of unease or apprehension. Therefore, let fidelity serve as the guiding principle in the pursuit of actualizing your desires in life.

A method to bolster your faith is by engaging in the practice of reciting affirmations on a daily basis. Affirmations are constructive declarations that reside within the depths of your subconscious. Presented herein are a collection of affirmations suitable for daily recitation, intended to fortify your conviction in the universe's inherent ability to furnish all desired outcomes unto you:

I hold a firm belief in the principle of the law of attraction.

The principle of attraction is exerting its influence on my life.

I am of the conviction that the universe is supportive of me.

Irrespective of my present situation, I maintain unwavering faith in the potential of my aspirations.

I opt to place my belief in something greater.

I expect success.

Each passing day brings me nearer to the realization of my aspirations.

The universe functions as a beneficent entity that fulfills my boundless desires.

I believe.

Certainly, you have the ability to construct your own affirmations. It is crucial to select affirmations that align with your personal comfort level. Do not recite these affirmations with a sense of obligation or burden. It is imperative to recite these affirmations with unwavering faith and resolute conviction. Additionally, it is imperative that you place your trust in the superior design of the cosmos, which surpasses any personal strategies or agendas. At times, one may not obtain their desired outcome; nevertheless, they shall undoubtedly receive an enhanced alternative. Therefore, remain calm and have faith in the belief that the cosmos will manifest all that you yearn and aspire for.

One must place their trust in the cosmic order, understanding that they are precisely situated in the most fitting place. One must exude the resonance of steadfast belief, and in due course, the cosmos will align with one's convictions.

www.ingramcontent.com/pod-product-compliance
Lightning Source LLC
Chambersburg PA
CBHW071129050326
40690CB00008B/1396